Mighty Mouse Gets A House For Christmas

By: Ann Carpenter

This story starts out a bit sad, but in the end it is happy. There once was a dog with no name, living in an animal shelter. She had lumps and bumps all over her body, and she was missing quite a lot of fur. She was all black. She seemed very old. She was very quiet and shy at the shelter. Quiet as a Mouse!

This dog did not have a house, but she was thankful for the shelter because she had a roof over her head.

This dog did not yet have a family, but she was thankful for the volunteers at the shelter with her. When the volunteers talked about her, they all said …..

…"She is quiet as a Mouse!" in fact, they began calling her "Mouse" as her name. Every day, they brought her toys and came to give her some love. Mouse especially loved when the volunteers loved on her, pet her, and took her on walks.

It was the month of December. Almost Christmas! All Mouse wished for was to have a family and a nice warm house!

During this time, there was a local pet store in town called Sea Paws that displayed an Angel Tree! Pictures of dogs and cats who were living at the shelter, adorned this tree. Customers could walk in, chose a photo off of the tree and come pick out toys and food for the particular pet that they were shopping for.

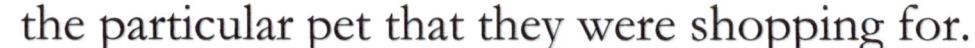

Mouse remained hopeful as she saw the other animals getting toys all around her. But she, at the same time, wondered why she had no toys or treats. Mouse was not aware that her photo was not hanging among the angel tree at Sea Paws, because the shelter did not make an ornament for her.

But one kind shelter volunteer noticed that her photo was not on the tree. The kind volunteer took on the special mission of being Mouse's temporary care-taker!

The next thing Mouse knew, was that she was getting a "freedom ride" from the shelter. The kind volunteer drove her home, gave her a bath, gave her kisses, and stroked her body gently. She even let Mouse sleep in a nice warm bed.

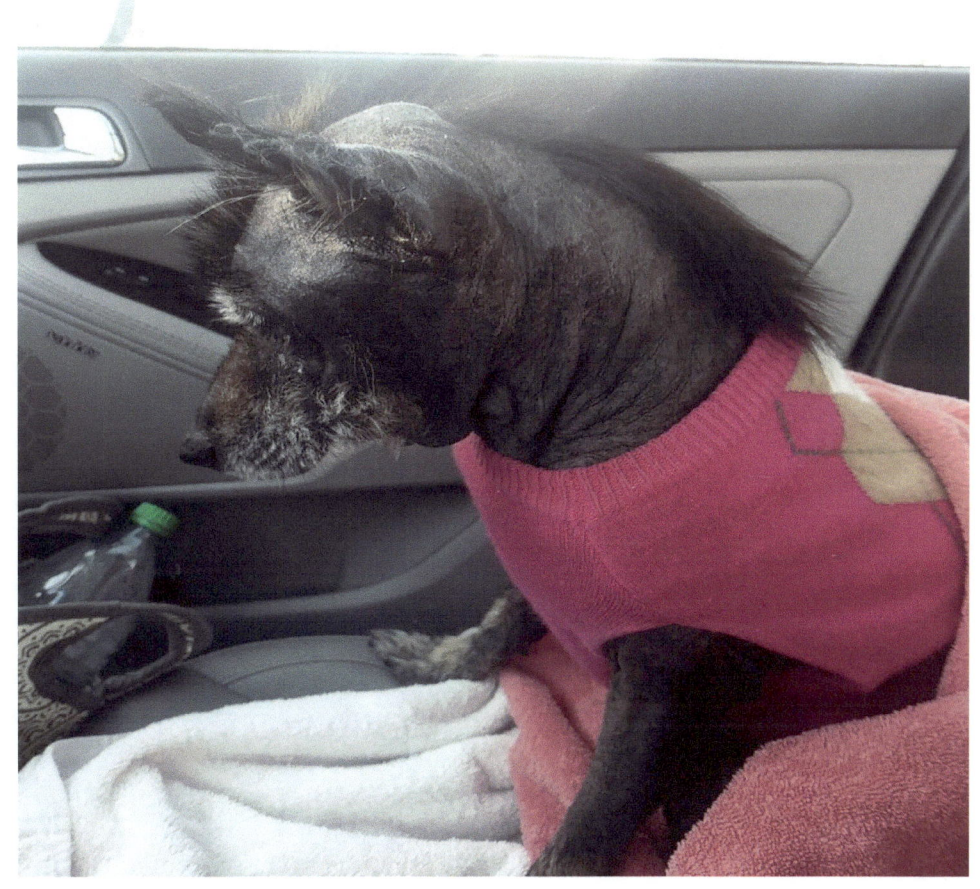

The kind volunteer took photos of Mouse on her phone, and was giving updates on social media about Mouse's story.

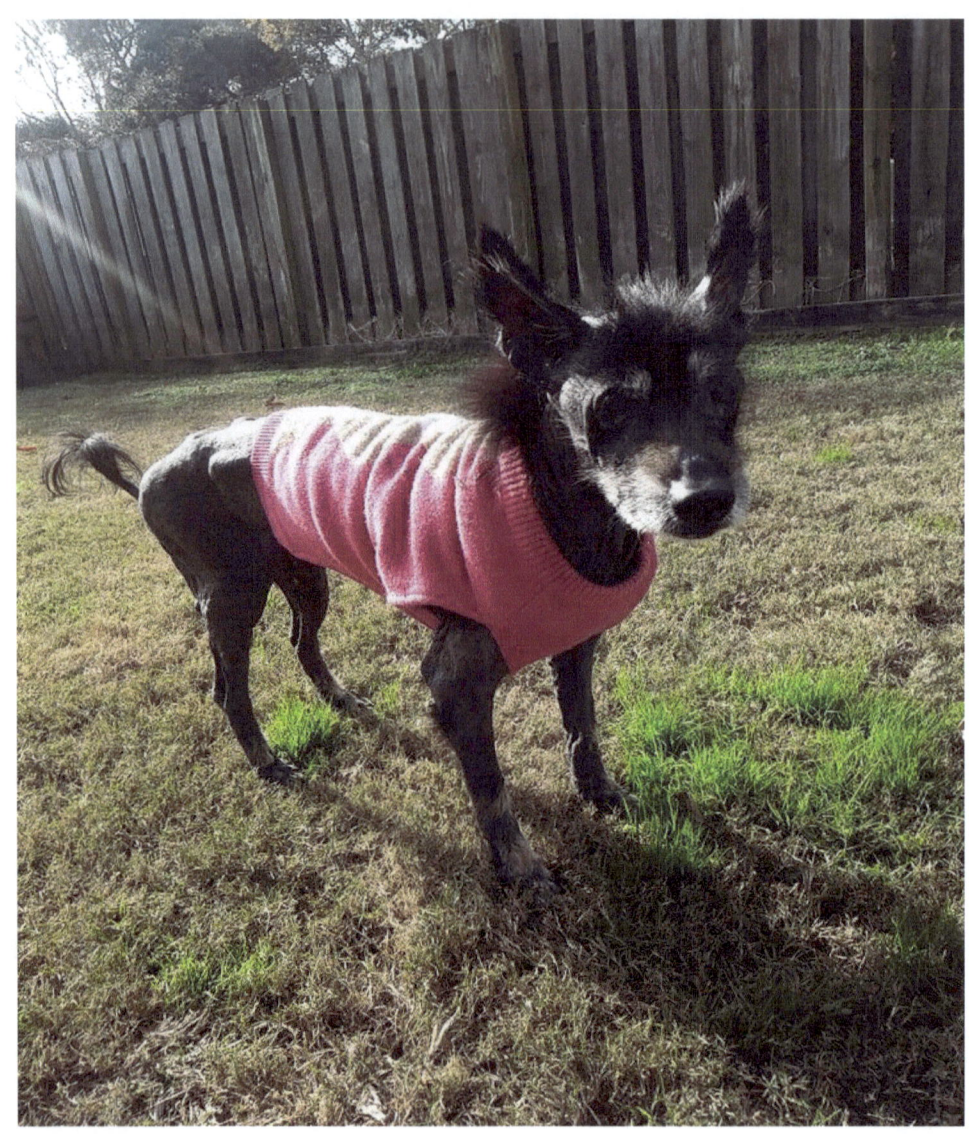

The next day, the kind volunteer brought Mouse to Sea Paws, where she met the two nice people who owned the store: A nice man and a nice woman.

At Sea Paws, Mouse saw the Angel Tree for the first time. She remembered wishing for a family for Christmas and she thanked the tree, in her heart, for the kind volunteer and the two nice owners of the Sea Paws store.

The two nice owners of Sea Paws took Mouse home with them that night and decided to be her foster parents and take care of her until she found the right forever family. While she was there, they took many photos of Mouse on their cell phone. They wanted to keep people up to date on life with Mouse.

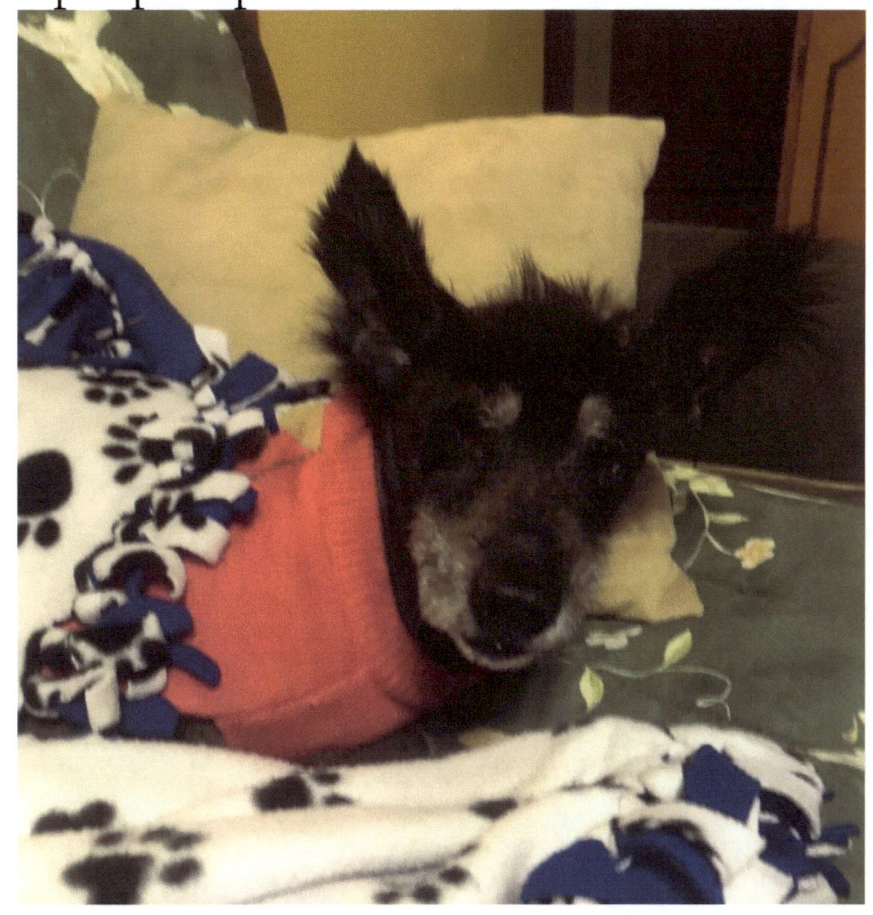

What Mouse was unaware of was what the Sea Paws owners, being her foster parents, meant. Being foster parents meant that they could not keep her forever, but would love her and keep her in their home until she could have the perfect forever family. Her foster parents worked tirelessly sharing Mouse's story on social media and in the store to ensure that Mouse would get a much-needed home.

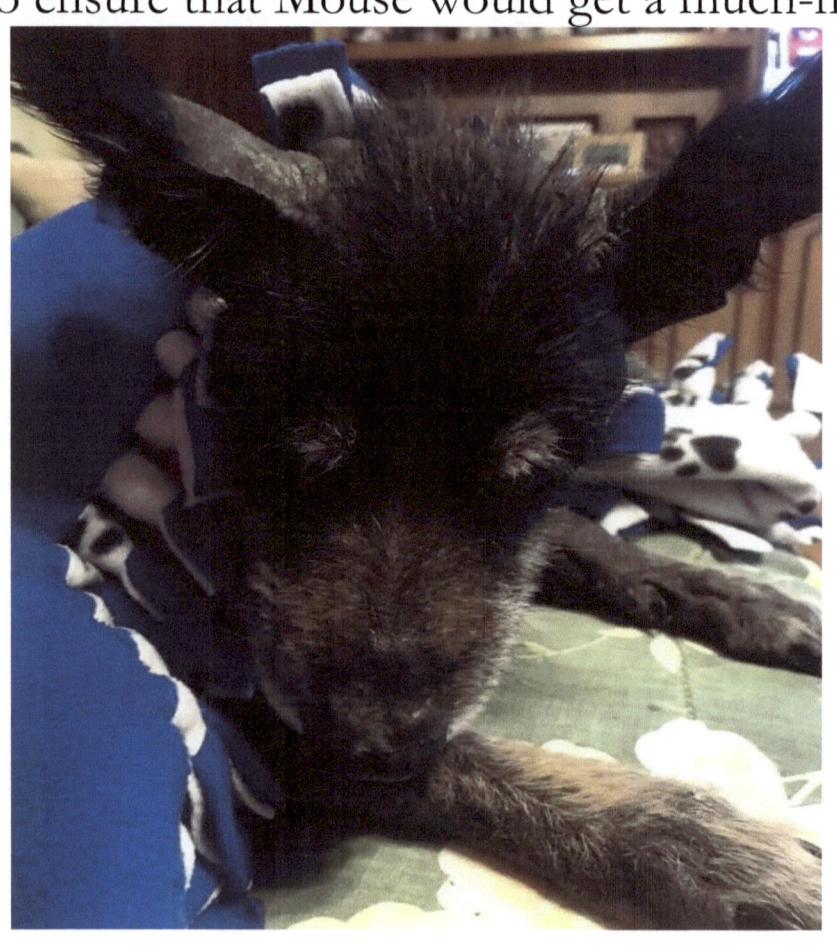

Mouse went to "work" at Sea Paws with her foster parents every day. At Sea Paws, she met so many nice people and received so much love in the form of hugs, kisses, pets and treats.

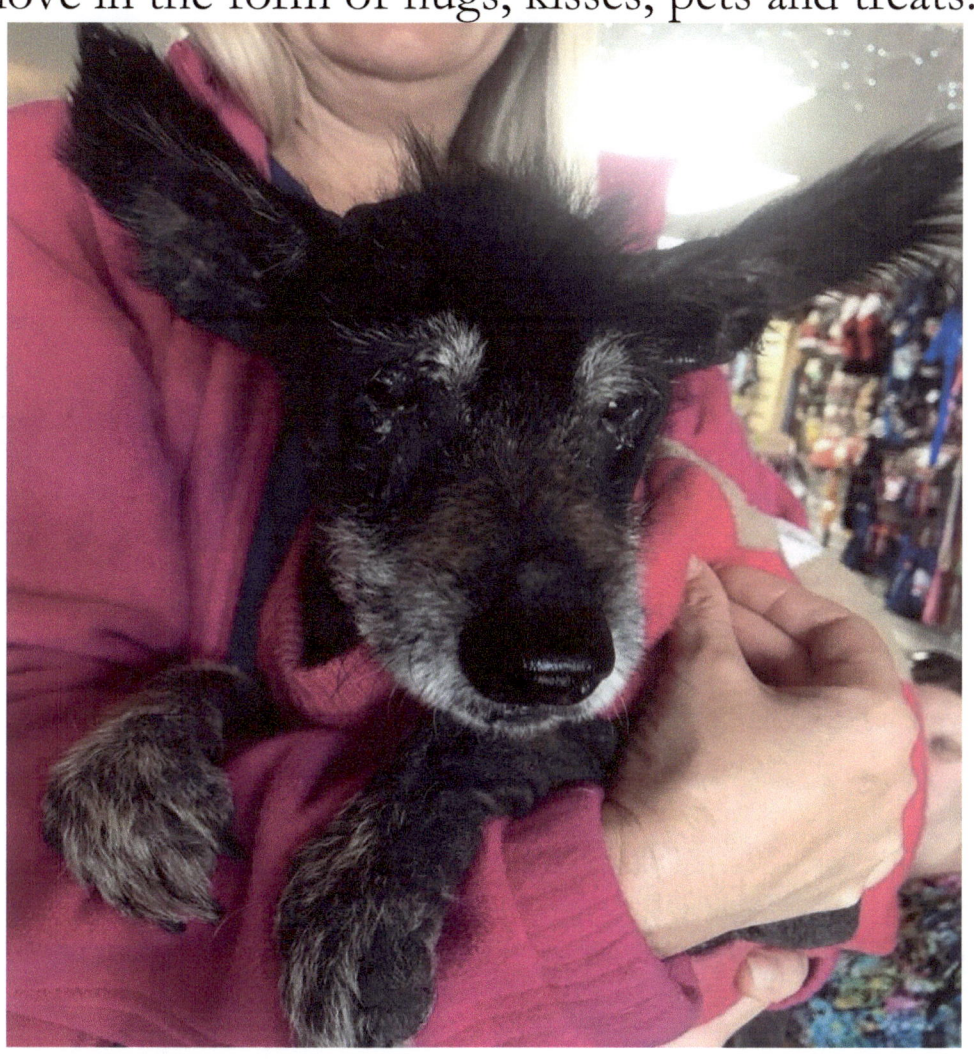

One day, a nice young lady came into Sea Paws and announced that she was there "to meet Mouse!"

Mouse's ears perked up!
"just to meet me?" she thought.
Mouse was not aware that her story and photos were being shared on Sea Paws web page.
Her fosters were strongly wishing that Mouse would get a home for the Holidays, as well.
The nice young lady gave Mouse hugs and kisses and held Mouse for a long while.

A few days later, the nice young lady who had come to meet Mouse at the store, arrived at her foster parents' home!
"How Odd!" Mouse thought, that the young lady would come to their store and then to their house.

The next thing Mouse knew, she was being loaded in the car with the nice young lady. The nice young lady drove her on a short car ride to another house!

At this new house, Mouse met her new brothers and sister, Jack, Bentley, Rex and Ella! They all sniffed Mouse and welcomed her into her new home.

In this new home, Mouse had her OWN bedroom. She could choose from one of two nice warm beds to sleep in. From the looks of all those toys and blankets, can you tell that she was spoiled from day one?

Mouse had already been with her new mom for two weeks. One night, mom began laying out sock-looking things near the crab pot Christmas tree. She laid out five of these sock-looking things. She also put out a plate of cookies and a glass of milk. She then tucked Mouse into her bedroom and brought her brothers and sister to bed.

The next morning, Mouse and her brothers and sister awoke to find the cookies and milk were gone! Each of the sock-looking things were filled with a ton of toys!

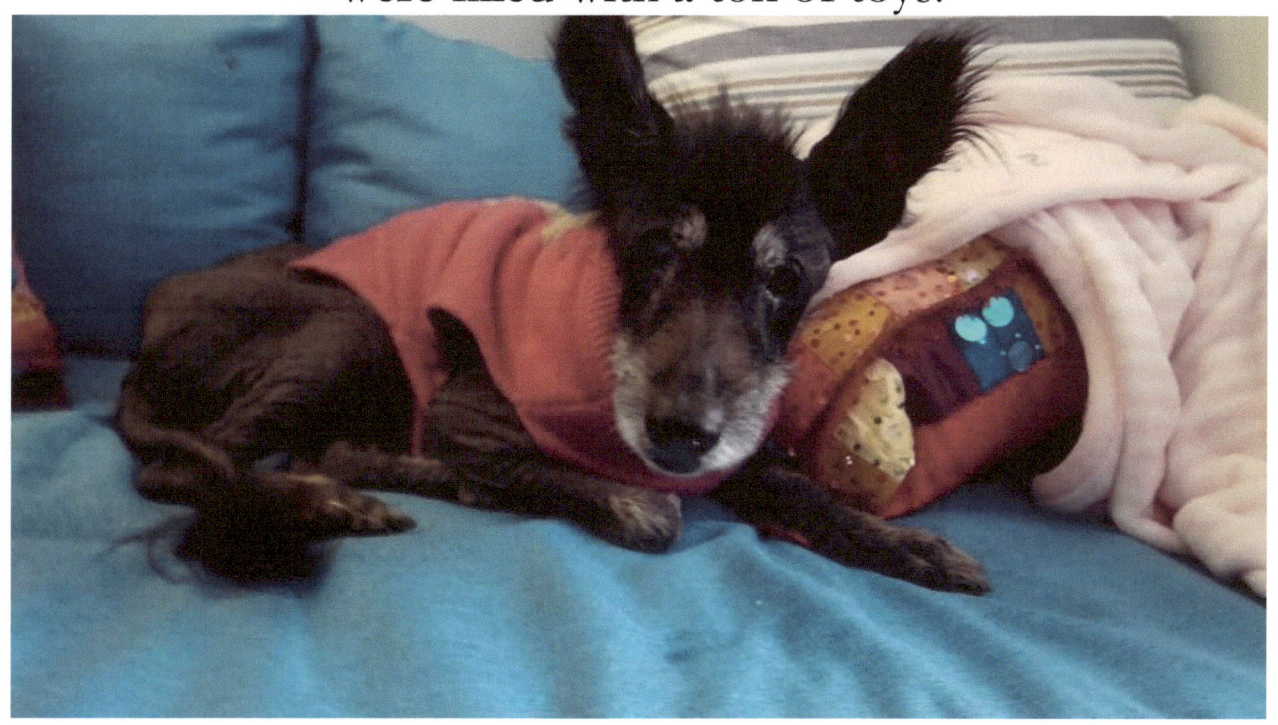

This morning was called "Christmas" and Mouse realized she had many things to be grateful for! Beyond new toys, Mouse had brothers and a sister whom she loved, an amazing Mom, and a nice warm home.

 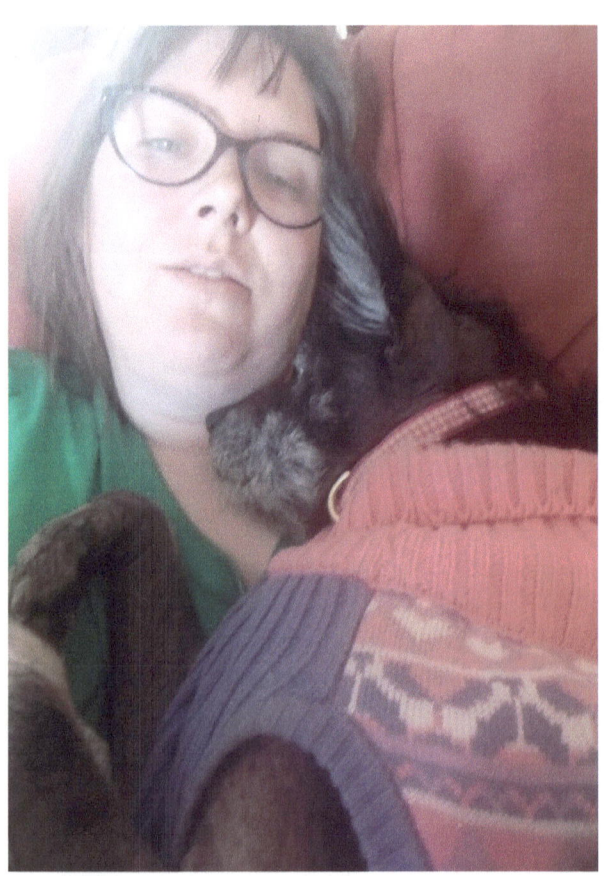

Once more, Mouse looked at the beautiful Christmas tree!
Yet again, in her heart, she thanked it for all she had….
Siblings, warmth, the love of a mommy….
And a nice home!
Mouse got a house for Christmas!

Adopt! Don't Shop!
½ of all proceeds will go toward donations for the Sea Paws Angel Tree During the Month of December

www.ingramcontent.com/pod-product-compliance
Lightning Source LLC
Chambersburg PA
CBHW041958150426
43193CB00003B/51